My *Canada*

PRINCE EDWARD ISLAND

By Sheila Yazdani

TABLE OF CONTENTS

A Crabtree Seedlings Book

Crabtree Publishing
crabtreebooks.com

School-to-Home Support for Caregivers and Teachers

This book helps children grow by letting them practice reading. Here are a few guiding questions to help the reader build his or her comprehension skills. Possible answers appear in red.

Before Reading:

• What do I know about Prince Edward Island?
  • *I know that Prince Edward Island is a province.*
  • *I know that Prince Edward Island has a lot of beaches.*

• What do I want to learn about Prince Edward Island?
  • *I want to learn which famous people were born in Prince Edward Island.*
  • *I want to learn what the provincial flag looks like.*

During Reading:

• What have I learned so far?
  • *I have learned that Charlottetown is the capital of Prince Edward Island.*
  • *I have learned that the Confederation Bridge is the longest bridge in the world that goes over ice-covered water.*

• I wonder why…
  • *I wonder why the provincial flower is the lady's slipper.*
  • *I wonder why you can fish for tuna at North Cape.*

After Reading:

• What did I learn about Prince Edward Island?
  • *I have learned that the sand at Singing Sands Beach sounds like it is singing when you walk on it.*
  • *I have learned that the provincial animal is the red fox.*

• Read the book again and look for the glossary words.
  • *I see the word **capital** on page 6, and the word **premier** on page 19. The other glossary words are found on pages 22 and 23.*

2

I live in Belfast. It is **rural**.

Point Prim **Lighthouse** is in Belfast. It is Prince Edward Island's oldest lighthouse.

Charlottetown

Prince Edward Island is a **province** in eastern Canada. The **capital** is Charlottetown.

Fun Fact: Charlottetown is the largest city in Prince Edward Island.

The provincial animal is the red fox.

We grow a lot of potatoes in Prince Edward Island. Some of them are used to make french fries.

Fun Fact: Prince Edward Island grows the most potatoes of any Canadian province.

My provincial flag has oak trees on it. At the top is a golden lion.

The Confederation Bridge is the longest bridge in the world that goes over ice-covered water.

Fun Fact: There are more than 300 kinds of birds at Prince Edward Island National Park, including piping plovers.

My family and I visit Prince Edward Island National Park. We go swimming at Cavendish Beach in the summer.

I like to learn about *Anne of Green Gables* at Green Gables Heritage Place.

I have fun at Singing Sands Beach. When you walk on the sand it makes a noise that sounds like singing!

Poet Mark Strand was born in Prince Edward Island. NHL head coach Gerard Gallant was also born in Prince Edward Island.

Fun Fact: Louis Henry Davies, a former **premier** of Prince Edward Island, was born in Charlottetown, Prince Edward Island.

I like to learn about history at the Acadian Museum.

Glossary

capital (CAP-ih-tuhl): The city or town where the government of a country, state, or province is located

island (IE-lind): Land that is surrounded by water

lighthouse (LIET-hows): A tower with a strong light that is used to guide ships

premier (pri-MYEER): The head of government of a province or territory

Charlottetown

province (PROV-ins): One of the large areas that some countries, such as Canada, are divided into

rural (RER-uhl): An area that is located outside towns or cities

Index

About the Author

Sheila Yazdani lives in Ontario near Niagara Falls with her dog Daisy. She likes to travel across Canada to learn about its history, people, and landscape. She loves to cook new dishes she learns about. Her favorite treat is Nanaimo bars.

Written by: Sheila Yazdani
Designed and Illustrated by: Bobbie Houser
Series Development: James Earley
Proofreader: Melissa Boyce
Educational Consultant: Marie Lemke M.Ed.

Photographs:
Alamy: gary corbett: p. 14-15; Michael DeFreitas: p. 17; Dorothy Alexander: p. 18 left; The History Collection: p. 19, 23; Norman Barrett: p. 20
Newscom: Tom Donoghue/Polaris: p. 18 right
Shutterstock: Elena Elisseeva: cover; Vadim.Petrov: p. 3, 22; Prashanth Bala: p. 4-5, 22-23; Media Guru: p. 6, 22-23; Darryl Brooks: p. 7; Tory Kallman: p. 8; Edgar Lee Espe: p. 9; Steve Photography: p. 10-11; New Africa: p. 11; Millenius: p. 12; Pi-Lens: p. 13; Harry Collins Photography: p. 14; Pascal Huot: p. 16; Jay Adams Company: p. 21

Crabtree Publishing

crabtreebooks.com   800-387-7650

Copyright © 2025 Crabtree Publishing

Printed in the USA/062024/CG20240201

Published in Canada
Crabtree Publishing
616 Welland Avenue
St. Catharines, Ontario
L2M 5V6

Published in the United States
Crabtree Publishing
347 Fifth Avenue
Suite 1402-145
New York, New York, 10016

Library and Archives Canada Cataloguing in Publication
Available at Library and Archives Canada

Library of Congress Cataloging-in-Publication Data
Available at the Library of Congress

Hardcover: 978-1-0398-3859-8
Paperback: 978-1-0398-3944-1
Ebook (pdf): 978-1-0398-4025-6
Epub: 978-1-0398-4097-3